Christmas Fairy Cooking

Leonie Pratt and Catherine Atkinson

Designed by Josephine Thompson
Illustrated by Molly Sage
Photographs by Howard Allman

Contents

Snowball truffles

To make about 15 truffles, you will need:

175g (6oz) white chocolate drops
25g (1oz) unsalted butter
50g (2oz) plain sponge cake
4 tablespoons desiccated coconut
small paper cases

Keep the truffles in a fridge, in an airtight container, and eat them within five days.

1. Fill a large pan a quarter full of water and heat it until the water bubbles. Then, remove the pan from the heat.

2. Put the chocolate drops and the butter into a heatproof bowl. Wearing oven gloves, carefully put the bowl into the pan.

Keep stirring until everything has melted.

3. After two minutes, stir the chocolate and butter until they melt. Wearing oven gloves, carefully lift the bowl out of the water.

4. Crumble the cake into fine crumbs. Add the crumbs to the chocolate mixture and stir everything well with a wooden spoon.

You could put the truffles in a gift box and give them to someone for Christmas.

5. Spread the coconut on a plate. Scoop up some of the chocolate mixture with a teaspoon and put it into the coconut.

6. Using your fingers, roll the chocolate mixture in the coconut to make a ball. When it is covered, put it into a paper case.

7. Make more truffles with the rest of the mixture. Then, put them onto a plate and put them in the fridge to chill for one hour.

Mini raspberry swirls

To make about 40 swirls, you will need:

225g (8oz) ready-made puff pastry, cut from a block and taken out of the fridge 20 minutes before you start.
icing sugar for dusting a work surface
3 tablespoons raspberry jam
1 tablespoon of caster sugar

You will need to heat your oven to 200°C, 400°F, gas mark 6 in step 6.

❄ Keep the swirls in an airtight container and eat them within five days.

Cut inside the lines.

1. Draw around a baking tray on baking parchment. Cut out the shape and put it in the tray. Then, do the same with another tray.

2. Dust some icing sugar over a clean work surface and on a rolling pin. Roll out the pastry to a square as wide as the rolling pin.

3. Use a sharp knife to trim the edges so that they are straight. Then, cut the pastry down the middle to make two rectangles.

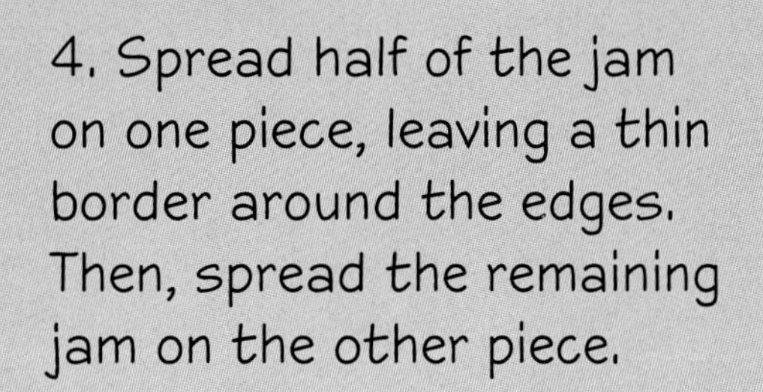

4. Spread half of the jam on one piece, leaving a thin border around the edges. Then, spread the remaining jam on the other piece.

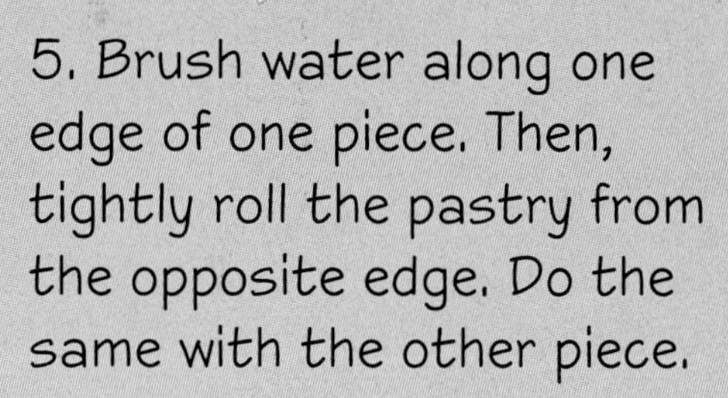

5. Brush water along one edge of one piece. Then, tightly roll the pastry from the opposite edge. Do the same with the other piece.

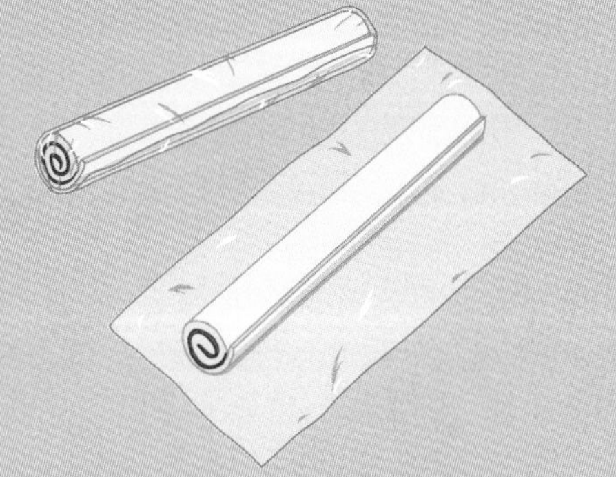

6. Wrap the rolls in plastic foodwrap and put them in the fridge to chill for 30 minutes. Meanwhile, turn on your oven.

7. Unwrap the rolls of pastry and put them on a chopping board. Cut the rolls into slices about as wide as your finger.

8. Put the swirls on the baking trays, leaving spaces in between them. Then, sprinkle half the caster sugar over them.

Wear oven gloves.

9. Bake the swirls for 10-12 minutes, until the pastry is golden. Then, carefully take the swirls out of the oven.

10. Sprinkle the rest of the caster sugar over the swirls. After five minutes, move them onto a wire rack to cool.

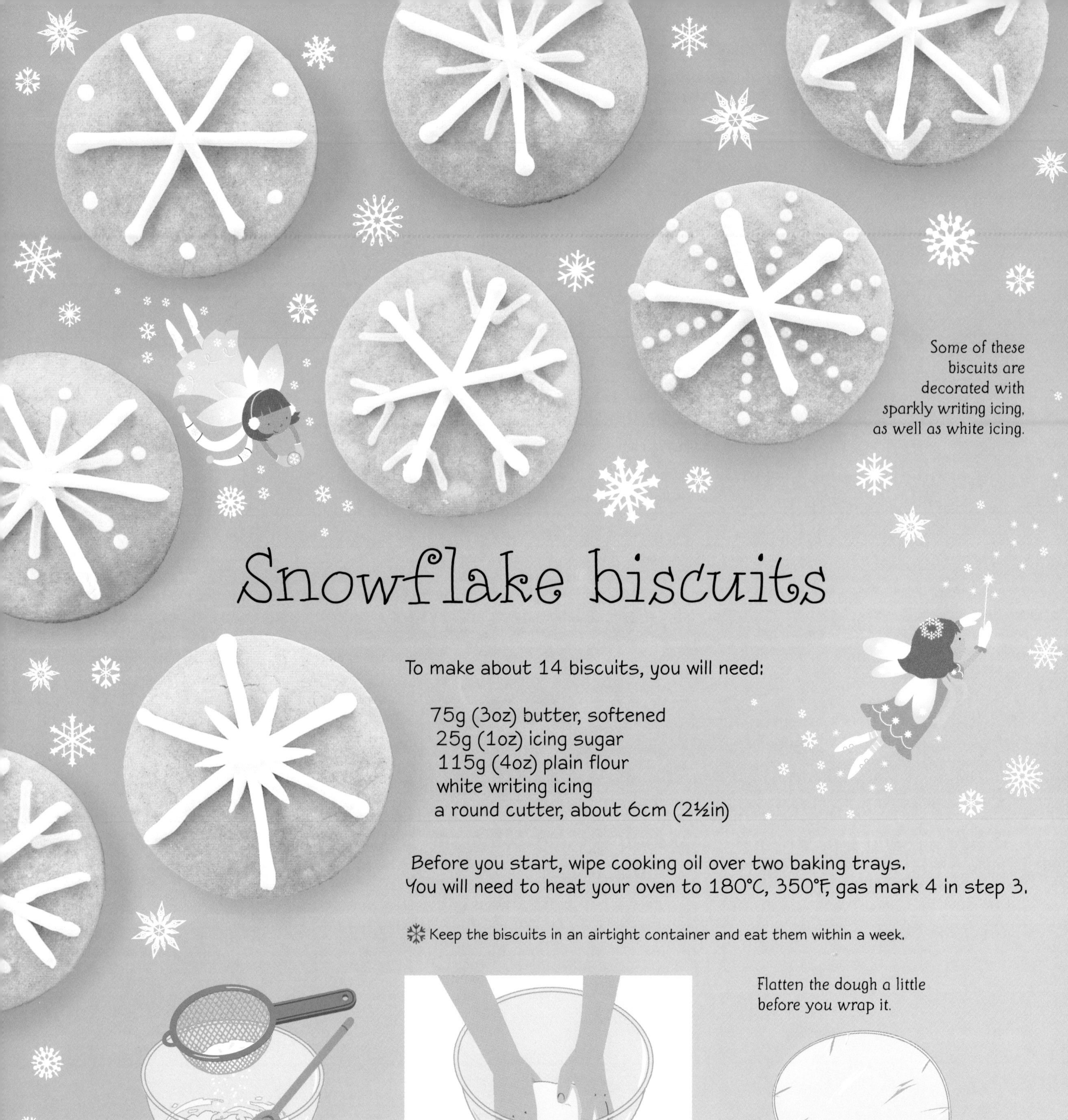

Some of these biscuits are decorated with sparkly writing icing, as well as white icing.

Snowflake biscuits

To make about 14 biscuits, you will need:

75g (3oz) butter, softened
25g (1oz) icing sugar
115g (4oz) plain flour
white writing icing
a round cutter, about 6cm (2½in)

Before you start, wipe cooking oil over two baking trays.
You will need to heat your oven to 180°C, 350°F, gas mark 4 in step 3.

Keep the biscuits in an airtight container and eat them within a week.

Flatten the dough a little before you wrap it.

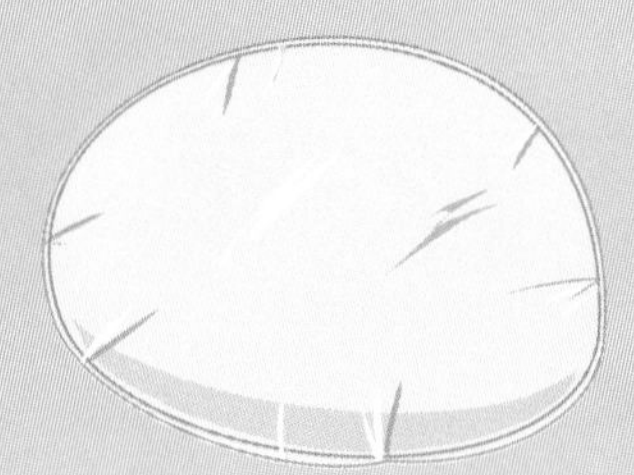

1. Put the butter into a large bowl. Stir it until it is creamy. Sift the icing sugar into the bowl and stir it in, until the mixture is smooth.

2. Sift the flour into the bowl and stir it in with a wooden spoon. Then, using your hands, squeeze the mixture to make a dough.

3. Wrap the dough in plastic foodwrap and put it in a fridge for 30 minutes. While the dough chills, turn on your oven.

Try drawing different patterns on some of the biscuits.

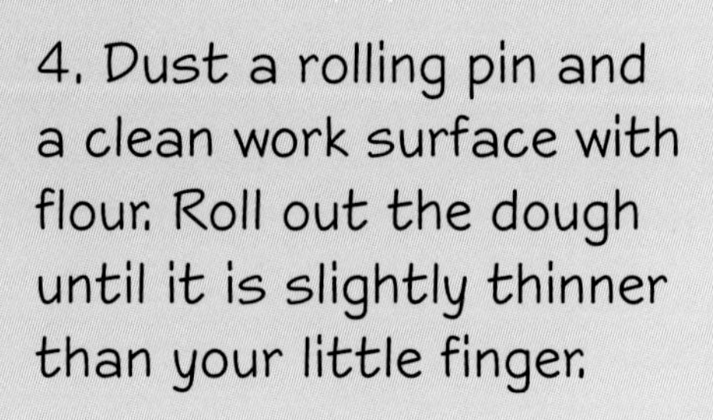

4. Dust a rolling pin and a clean work surface with flour. Roll out the dough until it is slightly thinner than your little finger.

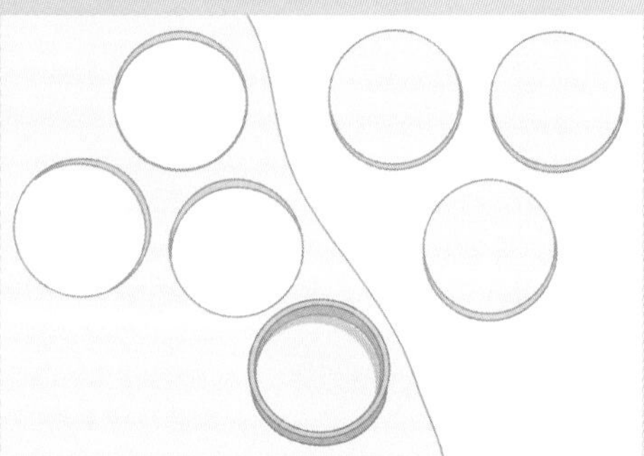

5. Cut out lots of circles with the cutter. Then, squeeze the scraps into a ball and roll it out again. Cut out more circles.

6. When you have used all the dough, put the circles onto the baking trays. Then, bake the biscuits for 10-12 minutes.

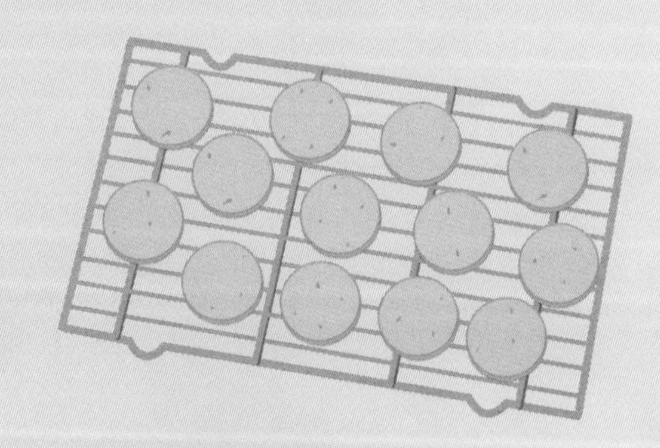

7. Leave the biscuits on the baking trays for two minutes. Then, move them onto a wire rack with a spatula and let them cool.

8. Draw a line down the middle of one biscuit with white writing icing. Draw two more lines crossing over the first one, like this.

9. Make a snowflake by adding small lines of writing icing across the ends of the lines. Then, decorate all the other biscuits, too.

Jewelled fairy muffins

To make 12 muffins, you will need:

150ml (¼ pint) milk
65g (2½oz) plain chocolate drops
150g (5oz) caster sugar
65g (2½oz) butter, softened
1 medium egg
150g (5oz) self-raising flour
paper muffin cases
a 12-hole baking or muffin tray

For decorating:
75g (3oz) butter, softened
175g (6oz) icing sugar, sifted
a few drops of vanilla essence
2 teaspoons milk
small sweets and sugar sprinkles

Before you start, put 12 paper muffin cases into the baking tray and heat your oven to 190°C, 375°F, gas mark 5.

Keep the muffins in an airtight container and eat them within two days.

Keep stirring so that the mixture does not stick.

1. Put the milk, chocolate drops and 50g (2oz) of the caster sugar into a small pan. Then, gently heat the pan on a low heat.

2. When the chocolate has melted, and the sugar has dissolved, take the pan off the heat. Then, leave the mixture to cool.

3. Put the butter into a large bowl and stir until it is creamy. Add the rest of the sugar and stir the mixture until it is fluffy.

4. Break the egg into a mug and stir it with a fork. Add half of the egg to the bowl and stir it in, then add the rest and stir that in, too.

5. Sift half of the flour through a sieve into the bowl. Pour in half of the chocolate mixture and stir it in with a wooden spoon.

6. Sift in the remaining flour and add the rest of the chocolate mixture. Mix everything well and spoon the mixture into the cases.

7. Bake the muffins for 15 minutes, then take them out of the oven. After two minutes, put them onto a wire rack to cool.

8. For the icing, put the butter into a large bowl and stir it until it is creamy. Add some of the icing sugar and stir it in.

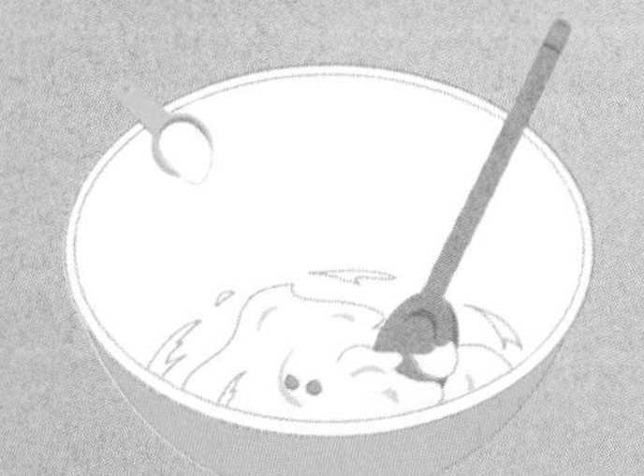

9. Add the rest of the sugar, a little at a time, stirring it in well. Then, add the vanilla essence and milk, and stir them in.

10. Peel the paper cases off the muffins. Use a blunt knife to spread icing on top of them, then press on sweets to decorate.

Christmas fairy kisses

To make about 20 biscuits, you will need:

100g (4oz) butter, softened
1 teaspoon of vanilla essence
50g (2oz) icing sugar
100g (4oz) plain flour
25g (1oz) cornflour
25g (1oz) desiccated coconut
about 2 tablespoons of seedless raspberry jam

Before you start, wipe two baking trays with cooking oil.
Heat your oven to 180°C, 350°F, gas mark 4.

❄ Keep the biscuits in an airtight container and eat them within five days.

1. Put the butter into a large bowl and stir it until it is creamy. Then, add the vanilla essence and stir it in.

2. Sift the icing sugar through a sieve into the bowl. Then, stir the mixture well until it is smooth and creamy.

3. Sift the flour and the cornflour into the bowl. Then, add the coconut and stir everything well to make a soft dough.

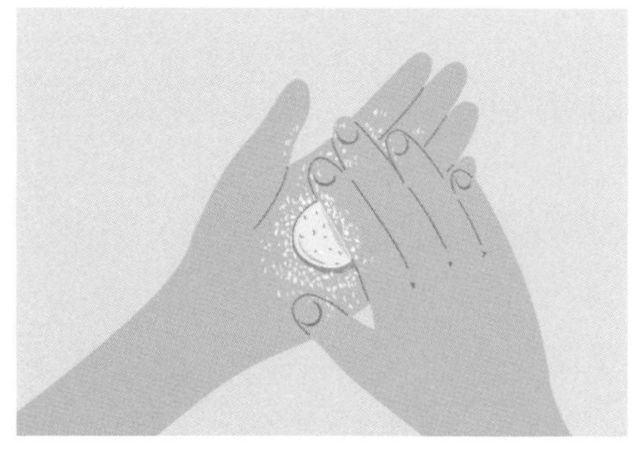

4. Rub some flour on your hands. Then, scoop up a little of the dough with a teaspoon and roll it into a smooth ball.

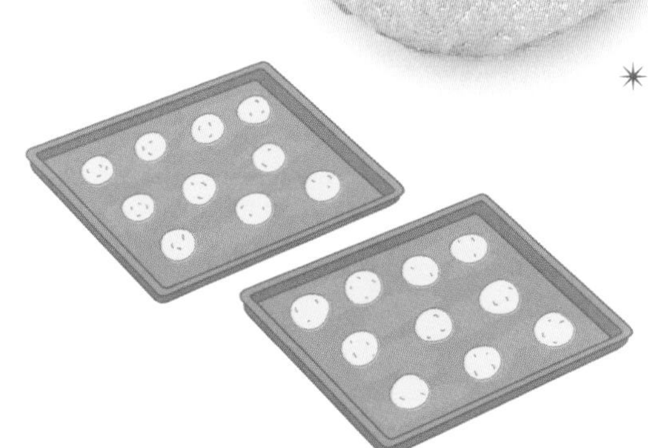

5. Make more balls and put them on the greased baking trays. Leave spaces between the balls, because they spread as they cook.

6. Push your little finger into the middle of each ball, to make a hollow. Push it in up to the first knuckle, like this.

7. Bake the biscuits for 12-14 minutes. Carefully lift them out of the oven, then leave them to cool on the trays.

8. When the biscuits have cooled, sift a little icing sugar over them. Then, use a teaspoon to fill the holes with jam.

Iced fairy crowns

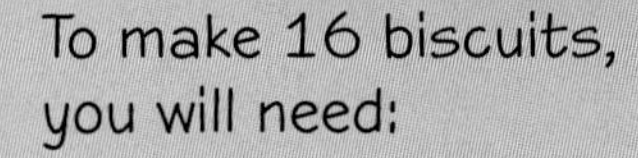

To make 16 biscuits,
you will need:

50g (2oz) butter
3 tablespoons golden syrup
175g (6oz) self-raising flour
half a teaspoon of ground cinnamon
half a teaspoon of bicarbonate of soda
1 tablespoon of light soft brown sugar
2 tablespoons milk
writing icing and sweets for decorating

Before you start, wipe cooking oil over two baking trays. Heat your oven to 180°C, 350°F, gas mark 4 in step 5.

❄ Keep the biscuits in an airtight container and eat them within three days.

1. Cut the butter into cubes and put them into a small pan. Add the golden syrup, then gently heat the pan on a low heat.

2. Stir the mixture every now and then, until it has just melted. Then, take the pan off the heat and let it cool for three minutes.

3. Sift the flour, cinnamon and bicarbonate of soda into a bowl and stir in the brown sugar. Make a hollow in the middle with a spoon.

4. Carefully pour the butter and syrup mixture into the hollow. Add the milk and stir everything until you have made a dough.

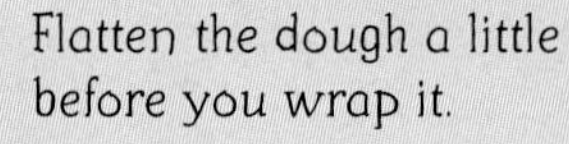

Flatten the dough a little before you wrap it.

5. Wrap the dough in plastic foodwrap and put it in the fridge for 15 minutes. While the dough is chilling, turn on your oven.

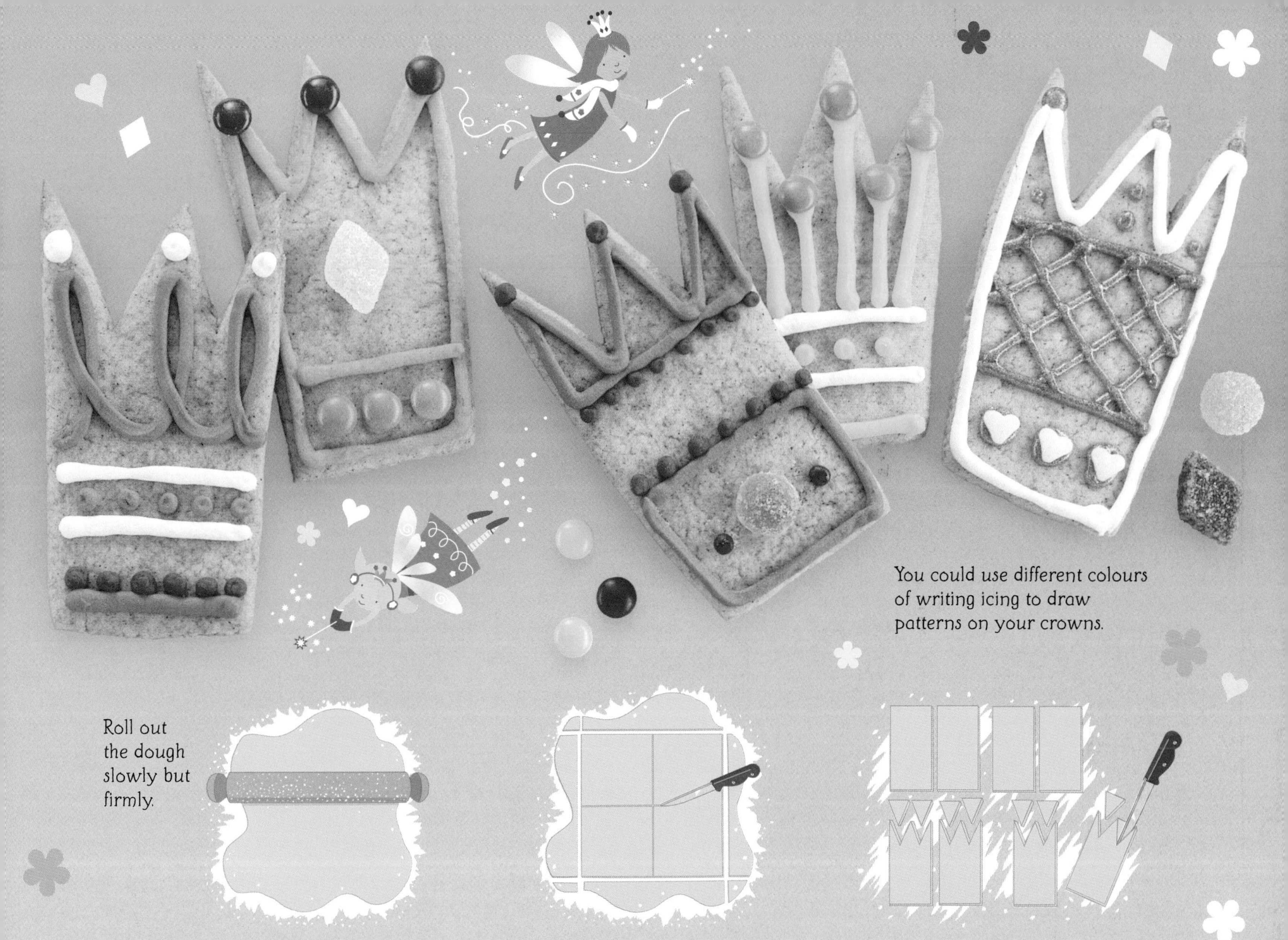

You could use different colours of writing icing to draw patterns on your crowns.

Roll out the dough slowly but firmly.

6. Dust a rolling pin and a clean work surface with some flour. Roll out the dough until it is half as thick as your little finger.

7. Cut off the wobbly edges of the dough with a sharp knife, to make a square. Then, cut the square into four pieces, like this.

8. Cut each piece in half, to make a rectangle. Then, make each rectangle into a crown by cutting out two small triangles at the top.

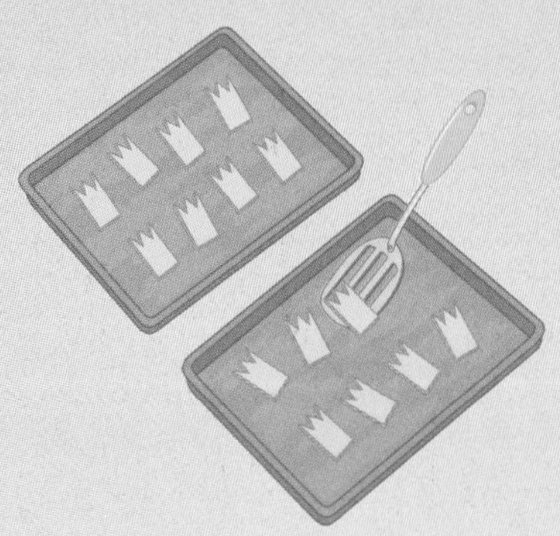

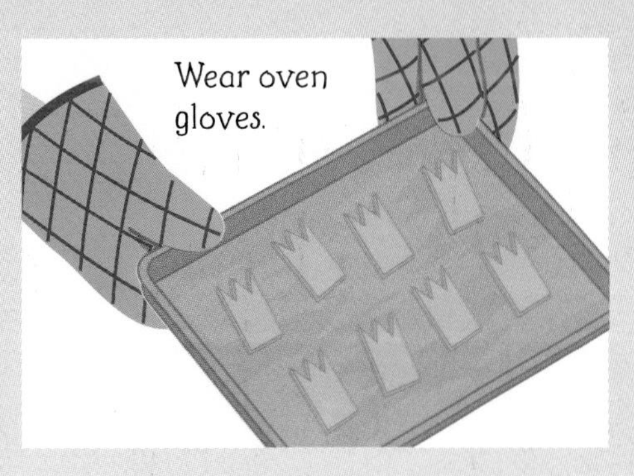

Wear oven gloves.

Stick on sweets with dots of icing.

9. Squeeze the scraps into a ball and roll it out again. Cut out more crowns, then put all of them onto the baking trays.

10. Bake the crowns for 8-10 minutes. Carefully lift them out of the oven and leave them on the baking trays for five minutes.

11. Lift the crowns onto a wire rack with a spatula, and let them cool. Then, decorate them with writing icing and sweets for jewels.

Snow cloud meringues

To make about 30 meringues, you will need:

2 eggs, at room temperature
100g (4oz) caster sugar
sugar sprinkles

Heat your oven to 110°C, 225°F, gas mark ¼, before you start.

Keep the meringues in an airtight container and eat them within a week.

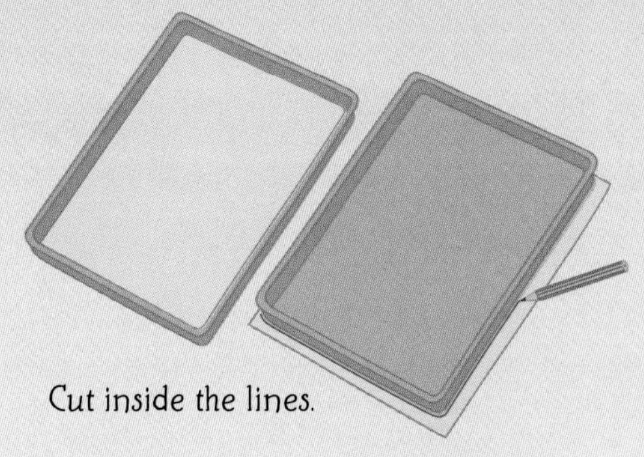

Cut inside the lines.

1. Draw around a baking tray on baking parchment. Cut out the shape and put it in the tray. Then, do the same with another tray.

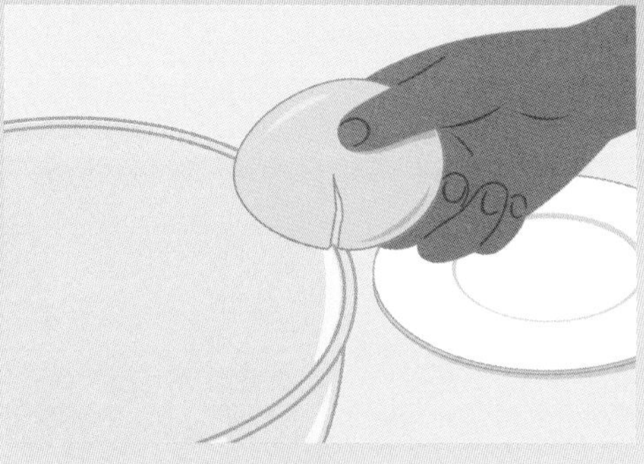

2. Carefully break one egg on the edge of a large bowl. Then, pour it carefully onto a saucer, so that the egg yolk doesn't break.

3. Hold an egg cup over the yolk and carefully tip the saucer over the bowl so that the egg white dribbles into it.

4. Repeat steps 2-3 with the other egg so that both egg whites are in the bowl. You don't need the egg yolks.

5. Whisk the egg whites with a whisk until they are really thick. They should form stiff points when you lift the whisk up.

6. Add a tablespoon of sugar to the egg white and whisk it in well. Whisk in the rest of the sugar a tablespoon at a time.

7. Scoop up a teaspoon of the meringue mixture. Then, use another teaspoon to push it off onto one of the baking trays.

8. Make more meringues until you have used all the mixture. Then, sprinkle a few sugar sprinkles over each one.

9. Put the meringues into the oven and bake them for 40 minutes. Then, turn off the oven, leaving the meringues inside.

10. After 15 minutes, carefully lift the baking trays out of the oven. Leave the meringues on the trays to cool.

Frosty fairy fudge

To make about 50 pieces of fudge, you will need:

350g (12oz) icing sugar
75g (3oz) unsalted butter
4 teaspoons milk
half a teaspoon of vanilla essence
75g (3oz) pink and white marshmallows
2 tablespoons sugar sprinkles
a shallow 18cm (7in) square tin

Keep the fudge in a fridge, in an airtight container, and eat it within a week.

1. Lay the tin on a piece of greaseproof paper. Draw around it with a pencil, then cut out the square, just inside the line.

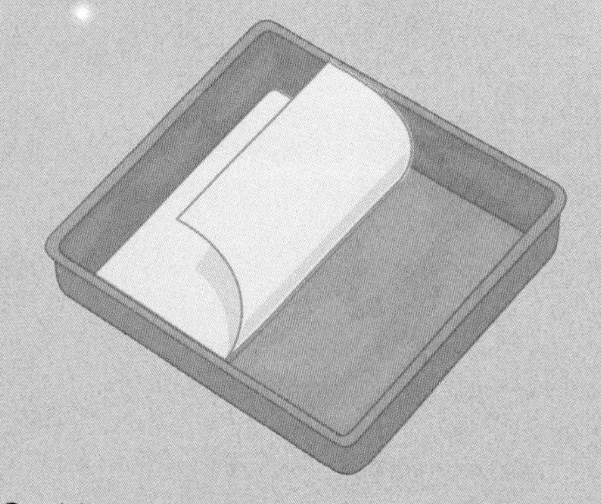

2. Use a paper towel to wipe cooking oil onto the sides and bottom of the tin. Press in the paper square and wipe it with oil.

Put the bowl to one side until step 6.

3. Sift the icing sugar through a sieve into a large bowl. Then, make a small hollow in the middle of the sugar with a spoon.

Use a pair of kitchen scissors.

4. Put the butter, milk and vanilla essence into a small pan. Then, cut the marshmallows in half and add them to the pan.

5. Gently heat the pan. Stir the mixture every now and then with a wooden spoon, until everything has melted.

6. Pour the mixture into the hollow in the middle of the sugar. Quickly stir everything together, until the mixture is smooth.

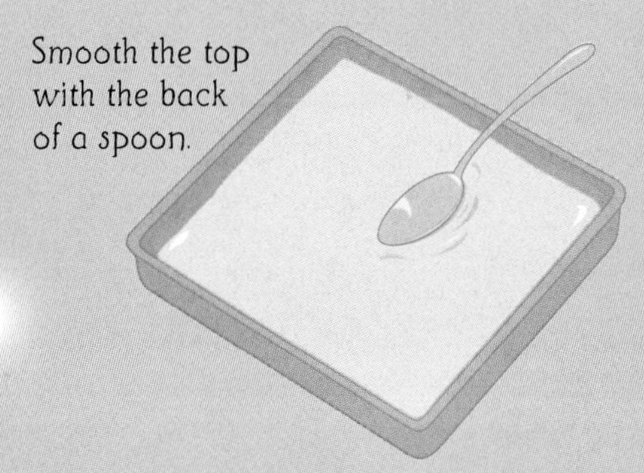

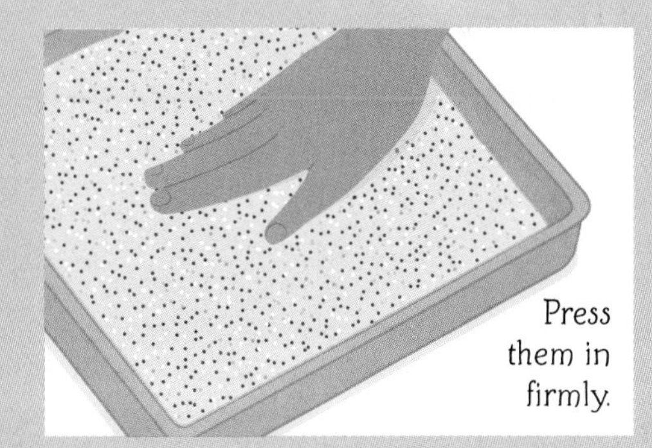

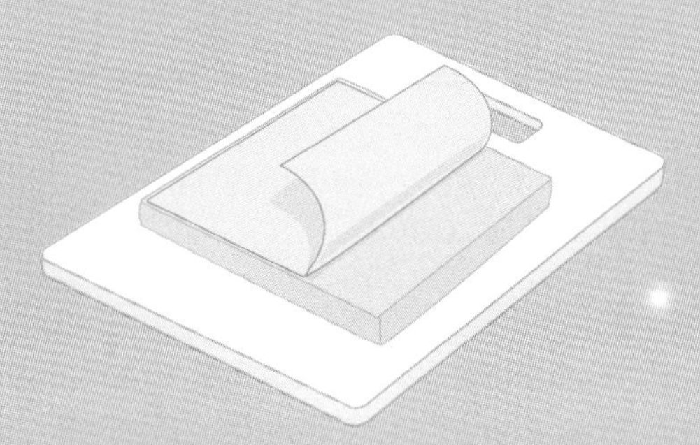

7. Pour the fudge into the tin and push it into the corners. Smooth the top, then sprinkle the sugar sprinkles over the fudge.

8. Use your fingers to press the sugar sprinkles into the fudge. When the fudge is cool, chill it in a fridge for two hours.

9. Loosen the edges of the fudge with a blunt knife. Then, carefully turn it out onto a board and remove the greaseproof paper.

10. Turn the fudge over and cut it into small squares. Put the fudge in an airtight container and chill it in the fridge for two more hours.

You could put the fudge into a cellophane bag and give it to someone as a present.

Christmas castle cake

For a cake which will serve 8-10 people, you will need:

175g (6oz) soft margarine
175g (6oz) caster sugar
3 tablespoons milk
1 teaspoon of vanilla essence
200g (7oz) self-raising flour
3 medium eggs
a shallow 18 x 28cm (7 x 11in) cake tin

For the decorations:
225g (8oz) icing sugar
3 tablespoons warm water
1 drop of pink food colouring
writing icing
small sweets

Heat your oven to 180°C, 350°F, gas mark 4, before you start.

❄ Keep the cake in an airtight container or cover it in plastic foodwrap, and eat it within three days.

1. Lay the cake tin on a sheet of greaseproof paper and draw around it. Then, cut out the shape, just inside the line.

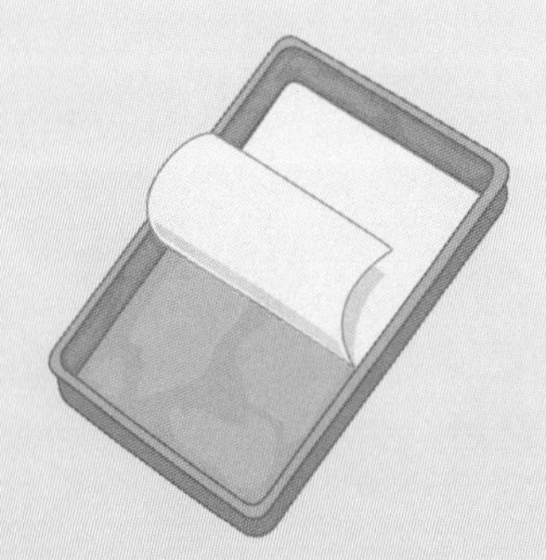

2. Use a paper towel to wipe some cooking oil on the bottom and sides of the tin. Press in the paper and wipe the top with oil.

3. Put the margarine and sugar into a large bowl. Mix the milk and vanilla essence together and pour them in. Then, sift the flour in, too.

4. Break the eggs into a mug and mix them with a fork. Add them to the bowl and stir the mixture until it is smooth and creamy.

5. Spoon the mixture into the tin and smooth the top. Bake it for 30-35 minutes, until the middle is springy when you press it.

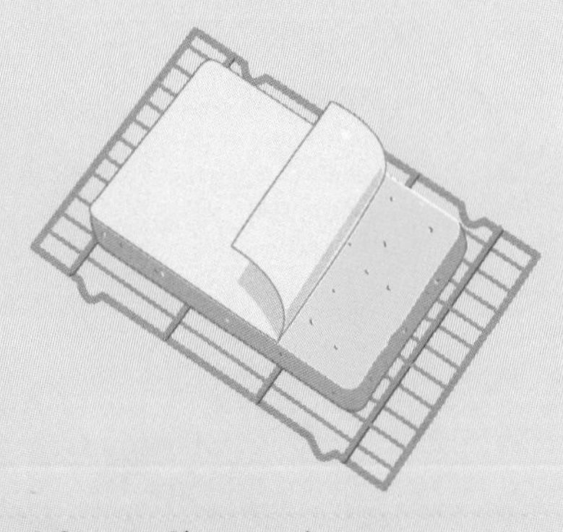

6. After five minutes, run a blunt knife around the cake. Turn it onto a wire rack and peel off the paper, then leave the cake to cool.

Put the strips on the board like this, to make three towers.

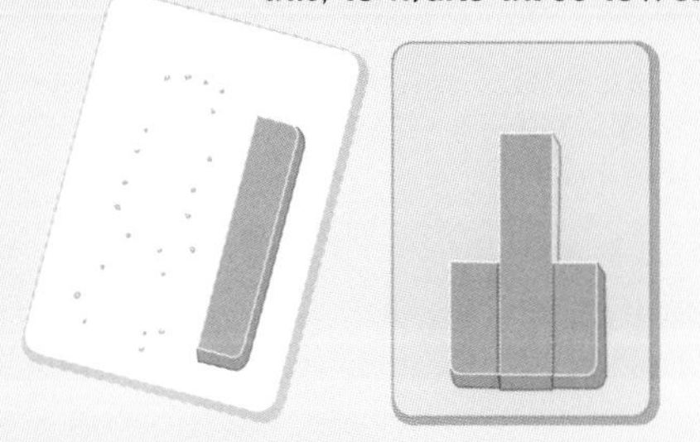

7. Put the cake on a board. Cut it into three strips and cut one strip in half. Move a long strip and the short strips onto another board.

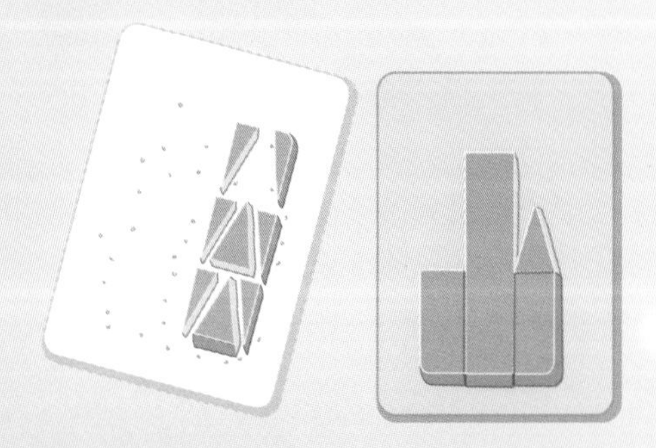

8. Cut the last strip into three equal pieces. Then, cut the pieces into tall triangles, for roofs. Put them on top of the towers.

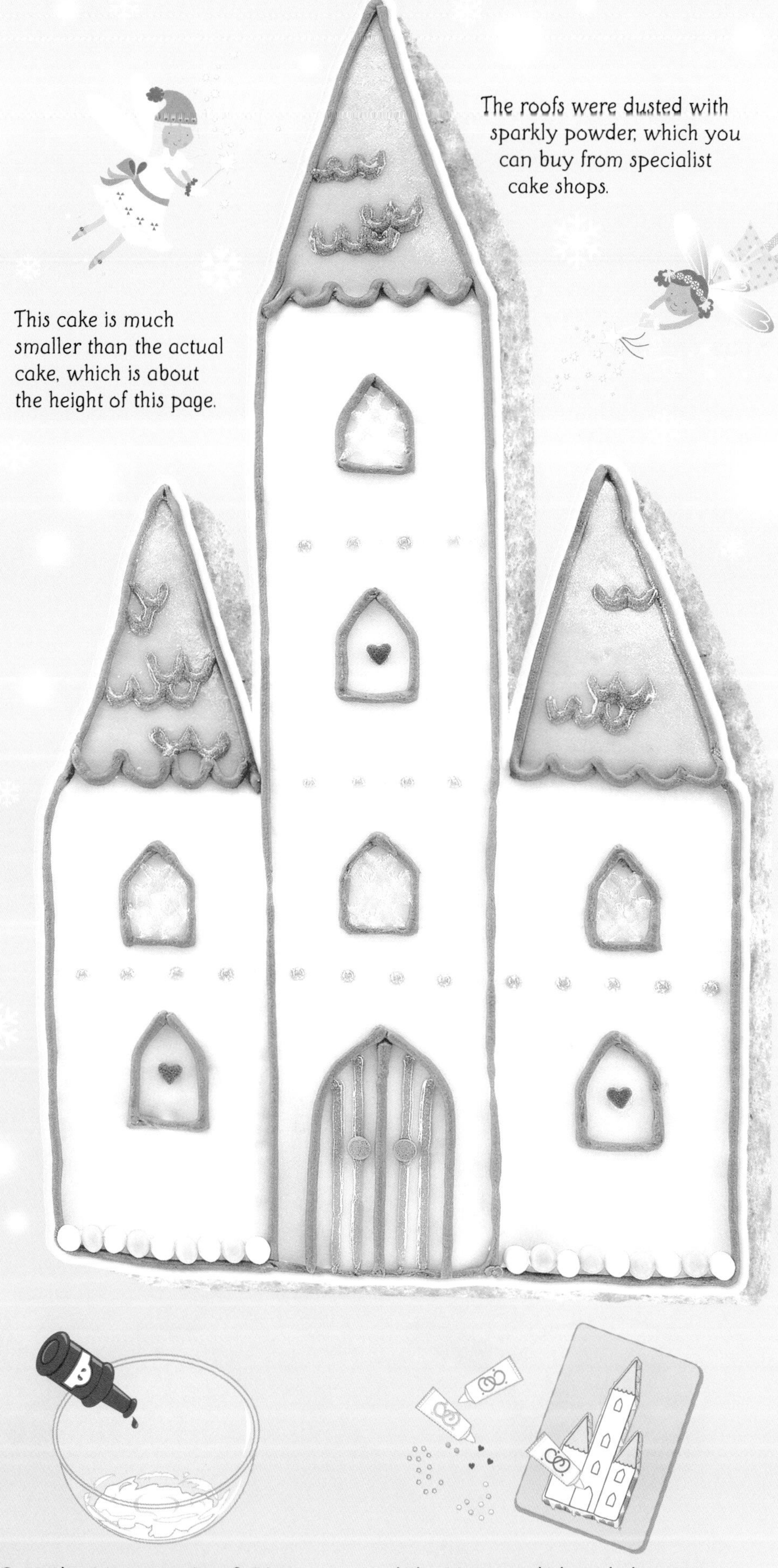

This cake is much smaller than the actual cake, which is about the height of this page.

The roofs were dusted with sparkly powder, which you can buy from specialist cake shops.

The icing should be smooth.

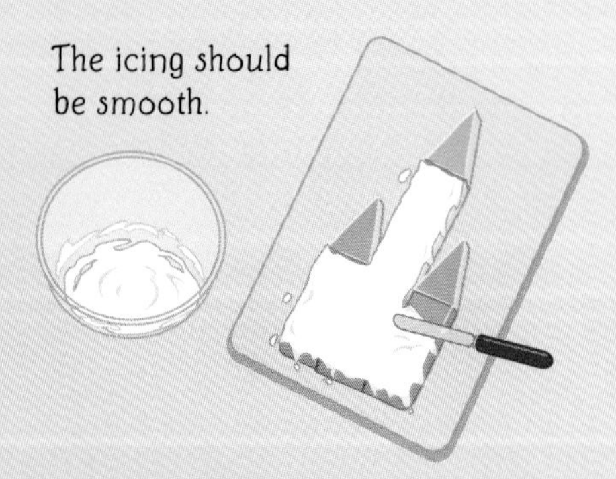

9. Sift 150g (5oz) of icing sugar into a bowl. Stir in two tablespoons of water, a little at a time, and spread the icing on the towers.

10. Mix the rest of the icing sugar with a drop of pink food colouring and one tablespoon of water. Spread it over the turrets.

11. Use writing icing to draw doors and windows on the castle. Add lines and dots of writing icing, then press on sweets.

Pretty pear pies

To make 12 pies, you will need:

375g (13oz) shortcrust pastry, taken out of the fridge 20 minutes before you start.
1 small orange
15g (½oz) butter
25g (1oz) soft light brown sugar
25g (1oz) dried cranberries
half a teaspoon of ground cinnamon
2 soft, sweet pears or four pear halves from a tin

milk for glazing
icing sugar for dusting
a 12-hole baking tray
a 7.5cm (3in) round cutter and a star-shaped cutter

Before you start, wipe cooking oil in the baking tray.
Heat your oven to 190°C, 375°F, gas mark 5 in step 5.

Keep the pies in an airtight container and eat them within five days.

You don't need the other half of the orange.

1. Grate half the rind from the orange using the fine holes on a grater. Cut the orange in half and squeeze the juice from one half.

2. Put the rind and one tablespoon of the orange juice into a pan. Then, add the butter, brown sugar, cranberries and cinnamon.

Cut tinned pears into small pieces.

3. Carefully peel the pears with a vegetable peeler. Cut them into quarters and cut out the cores. Then, cut the quarters into small pieces.

Keep stirring the mixture so that it doesn't stick.

4. Put the pieces of pear into the pan. Gently heat the mixture on a low heat for 10 minutes. Take it off the heat and let it cool.

Dust the rolling pin with flour, too.

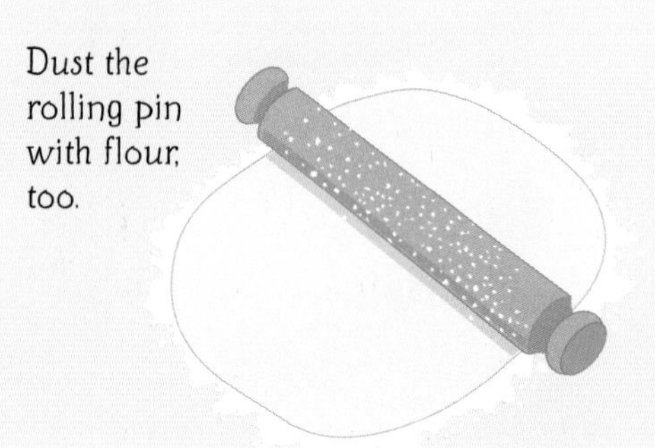

5. Turn on your oven. Dust a clean work surface with flour and roll out the pastry until it is slightly thinner than your little finger.

Cut the circles as close together as you can.

6. Cut 12 circles from the pastry with the round cutter. Then, press the scraps together to make a ball and put it to one side.

7. Press the circles into the pans in the baking tray. Then, put a heaped teaspoon of the pear mixture into each one.

8. Roll out the ball of pastry and cut out 12 stars with the star cutter. Lay the stars on the pies, then brush milk over them.

9. Bake the pies for 20 minutes, until they are golden. Then, lift them out and leave them in the tray to cool for 10 minutes.

10. Using a blunt knife, lift the pies onto a plate. Put a little icing sugar into a sieve and sprinkle the sugar over the pies.

Fairy fruit crispies

To make about 35 fruit crispies, you will need:

50g (2oz) dried apricots
40g (1½oz) puffed rice
75g (3oz) dried cranberries
1 tablespoon of golden syrup
50g (2oz) caster sugar
50g (2oz) butter
small paper cases

❄ Keep the crispies in a fridge, in an airtight container, and eat them within four days.

1. Use a clean pair of kitchen scissors to cut the dried apricots into small pieces so that they fall into a large bowl.

2. Add the puffed rice and the cranberries to the bowl. Then, mix everything together well with a wooden spoon.

Stir the mixture well.

3. Put the syrup, caster sugar and butter into a small pan. Gently heat the pan on a low heat, until everything has just melted.

Be careful – the mixture will be hot.

4. Turn the heat up to a medium heat and let the mixture cook for two minutes. Then, take the pan off the heat.

5. Leave the syrup in the pan to cool for five minutes. Then, carefully pour it over the puffed rice mixture.

6. Stir everything with a wooden spoon. Then, using a teaspoon, put a heaped spoonful of the mixture into each paper case.

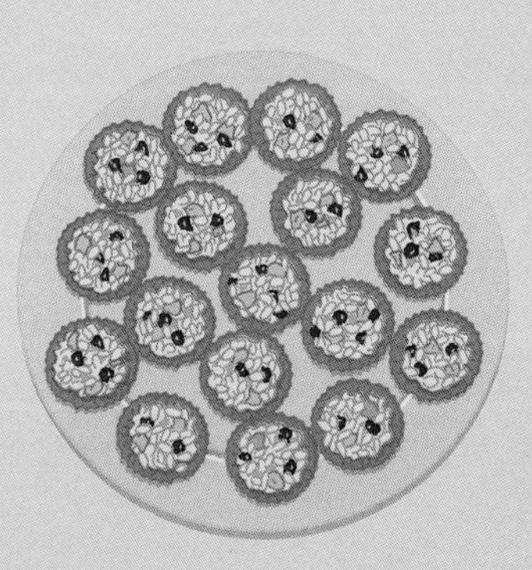

7. Put the crispies onto two plates and put them in a fridge. Leave them in there for one hour, until they have set.

Tiny Christmas cookies

To make about 65 tiny cookies, you will need:

50g (2oz) butter, softened
25g (1oz) icing sugar
quarter of a teaspoon of red food colouring
1 teaspoon of milk
quarter of a teaspoon of vanilla essence
75g (3oz) plain flour
little star and heart cutters

Before you start, wipe two baking trays with cooking oil.
Heat your oven to 180°C, 350°F, gas mark 4.

❄ Keep the cookies in an airtight container and eat them within a week.

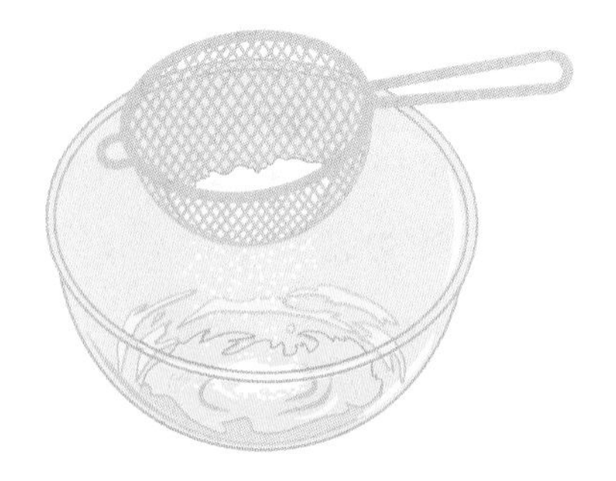

1. Put the butter into a bowl and stir it until it is creamy. Sift the icing sugar into the bowl and stir it in until the mixture is smooth.

2. Add the food colouring to the mixture and stir it in until the mixture is pink. Then, add the milk and the vanilla essence.

3. Sift the flour into the bowl and stir everything together. Then, use your hands to squeeze the mixture into a dough.

4. Dust a rolling pin and a clean work surface with flour. Roll out the dough until it is slightly thinner than your little finger.

5. Use the cutters to cut lots of shapes from the dough. Then, use a spatula to lift the shapes onto the baking trays.

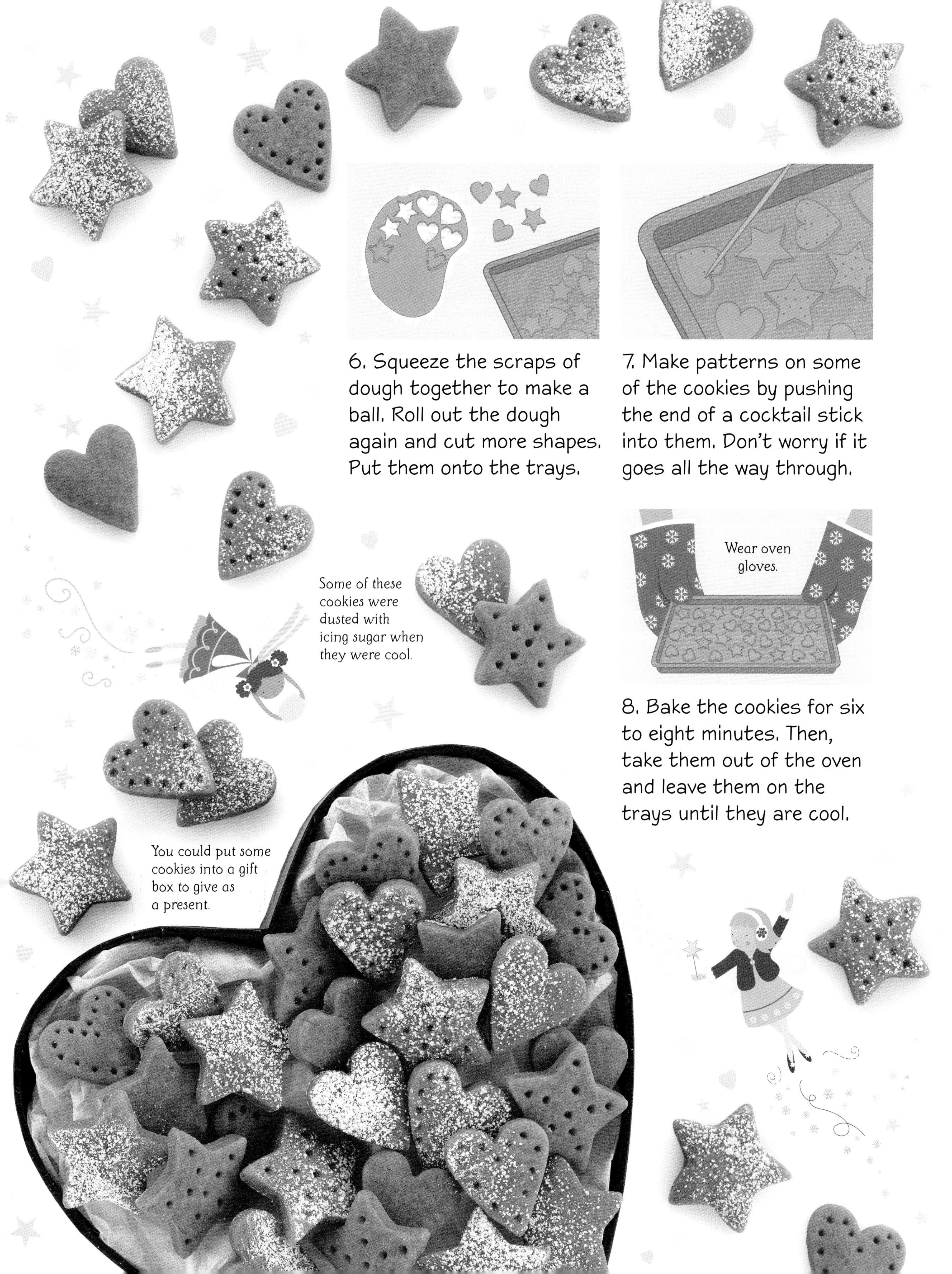

6. Squeeze the scraps of dough together to make a ball. Roll out the dough again and cut more shapes. Put them onto the trays.

7. Make patterns on some of the cookies by pushing the end of a cocktail stick into them. Don't worry if it goes all the way through.

Some of these cookies were dusted with icing sugar when they were cool.

8. Bake the cookies for six to eight minutes. Then, take them out of the oven and leave them on the trays until they are cool.

You could put some cookies into a gift box to give as a present.

Mini crispy buns

To make about 20 buns, you will need:

100g (4oz) soft margarine
50g (2oz) butter, softened
50g (2oz) light soft brown sugar
1 egg
1 teaspoon of vanilla essence
125g (5oz) self-raising flour
50g (2oz) corn flakes
200g (7oz) white chocolate drops
sugar sprinkles

Before you start, wipe two baking trays with cooking oil. Cut a large piece of greaseproof paper and put it on a chopping board, too. Heat your oven to 190°C, 375°F, gas mark 5.

These buns are best eaten on the day you make them.

1. Put the margarine and butter into a bowl and stir them until they are creamy. Add the sugar and stir the mixture until it is fluffy.

2. Break the egg into a cup and add the vanilla essence. Stir the mixture with a fork, then pour half of it into the bowl.

3. Stir in the egg mixture. Then, add the rest and stir that in, too. Sift the flour into the bowl and stir everything well.

4. Crush the corn flakes a little with your fingers and put them onto a plate. Scoop up a teaspoon of the mixture and put it on top.

5. Roll the mixture in the corn flakes to cover it. Then, put it on a greased baking tray and make more buns in the same way.

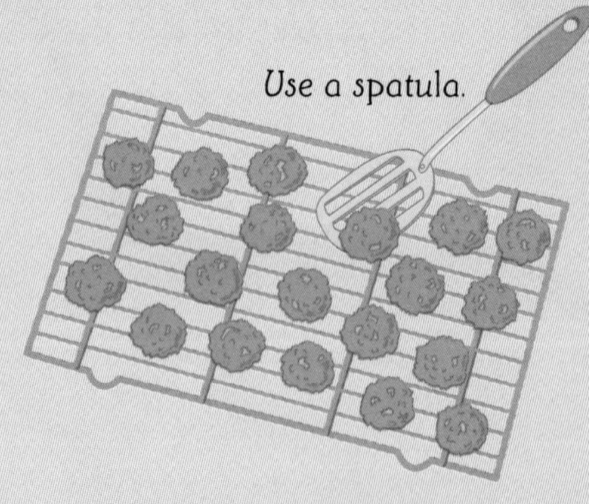

6. Bake the buns for 12-14 minutes. Leave them on the trays for two minutes, then lift them onto a wire rack to cool.

7. Fill a large pan a quarter full of water and heat it until the water bubbles. Then, remove the pan from the heat.

8. Put the chocolate drops into a heatproof bowl. Then, wearing oven gloves, carefully put the bowl into the pan of water.

9. After two minutes, stir the chocolate drops with a metal spoon until they have melted. Carefully lift the bowl out of the water.

10. Put the buns onto the chopping board. Then, spread a teaspoon of the melted chocolate over each bun.

11. Sprinkle sugar sprinkles on the buns. Then, put them in the fridge for 20 minutes, for the chocolate to set, or eat them straightaway.

Sparkly star biscuits

To make 20 biscuits, you will need:

3 tablespoons caster sugar
4 drops pink food colouring
75g (3oz) butter, softened
1 small lemon
25g (1oz) soft light brown sugar
3 tablespoons clear honey
1 medium egg
175g (6oz) plain flour
medium and small star cutters

Before you start, wipe two baking trays with cooking oil. Heat your oven to 180°C, 350°F, gas mark 4 in step 7.

❄ The biscuits need to be stored in an airtight container and eaten within five days.

1. Put the caster sugar into a bowl, then add the food colouring. Stir the sugar until it is pink. Then, spread it on a plate to dry.

Use the fine holes on the grater.

2. Put the butter into a large bowl and stir it until it is creamy. Then, grate the rind off the lemon and add the rind to the bowl.

3. Add the brown sugar and the honey to the bowl. Stir everything well with a wooden spoon, until the mixture is smooth.

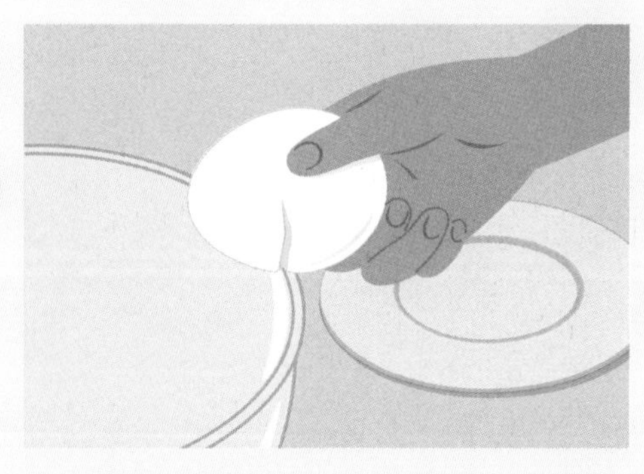

4. Carefully break the egg on the edge of a bowl. Then, pour the egg carefully onto a saucer, so that the egg yolk doesn't break.

Keep the egg white for later.

5. Put an egg cup over the yolk. Tip the saucer so that the egg white dribbles into a bowl. Then, stir the yolk into the honey mixture.

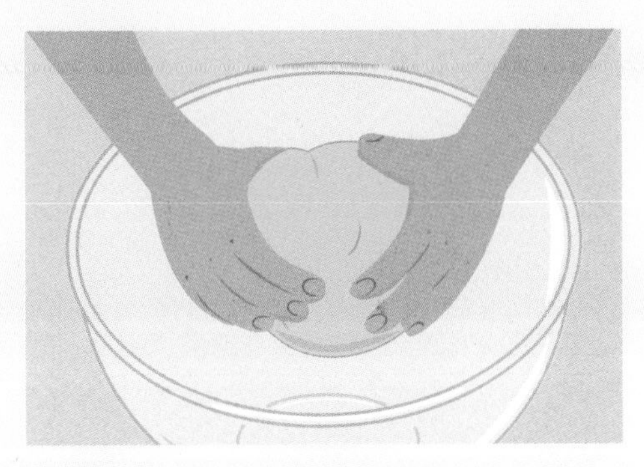

6. Use a sieve to sift the flour into the mixture. Stir it in, then squeeze the mixture to make a dough. Wrap it in plastic foodwrap.

7. Chill the dough in a fridge for 30 minutes. While it is chilling, heat your oven. Dust a clean work surface and a rolling pin with flour.

8. Roll out the dough until it is slightly thinner than your little finger. Then, use the medium cutter to cut out lots of shapes.

9. Use the small cutter to cut a star from the middle of each biscuit. Press the scraps into a ball, roll it out and cut out more stars.

10. Brush a little egg white over each star and sprinkle pink sugar on top. Then, use a spatula to lift the stars onto the baking trays.

11. Bake the biscuits for 8-10 minutes, until they are golden. Lift them out. After two minutes, lift them onto a wire rack to cool.

Christmas fairy crunchies

To make about 15 crunchies, you will need:

- 25g (1oz) glacé cherries
- 25g (1oz) rich tea or other plain biscuits
- 25g (1oz) white marshmallows
- 100g (4oz) white chocolate drops
- 25g (1oz) unsalted butter
- small paper cases

Keep the sweets in an airtight container, in a fridge, and eat them within a week.

1. Cut the cherries into tiny pieces and put them into a large bowl. Then, break the biscuits into lots of little pieces and add them, too.

2. Cut the marshmallows into small pieces, using a pair of kitchen scissors. Add them to the bowl and mix everything together.

3. Fill a large pan a quarter full of water and heat it until the water bubbles. Then, remove the pan from the heat.

4. Put the chocolate drops and the butter into a heatproof bowl. Wearing oven gloves, carefully put the bowl into the pan.

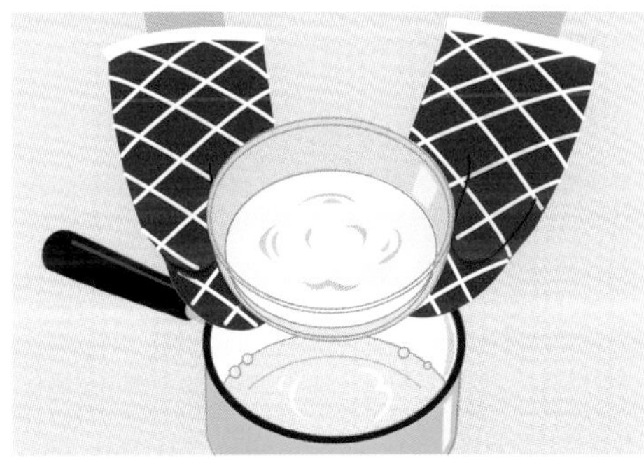

5. After two minutes, stir the mixture with a metal spoon. When everything has melted, carefully lift the bowl out of the pan.

6. Spoon the chocolate and butter mixture into the large bowl. Then, mix everything well with a wooden spoon.

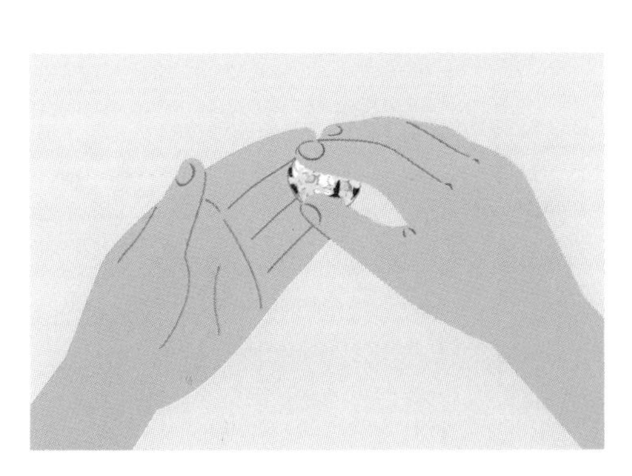

7. Use a teaspoon to scoop up some of the mixture. Shape the mixture into a ball with your fingers and put it into a paper case.

8. Make more balls in the same way, until you have used all the mixture. Then, press a dried cranberry onto the top of each one.

9. Put all the crunchies onto a large plate. Then, put the plate in a fridge and leave them to chill for two hours.

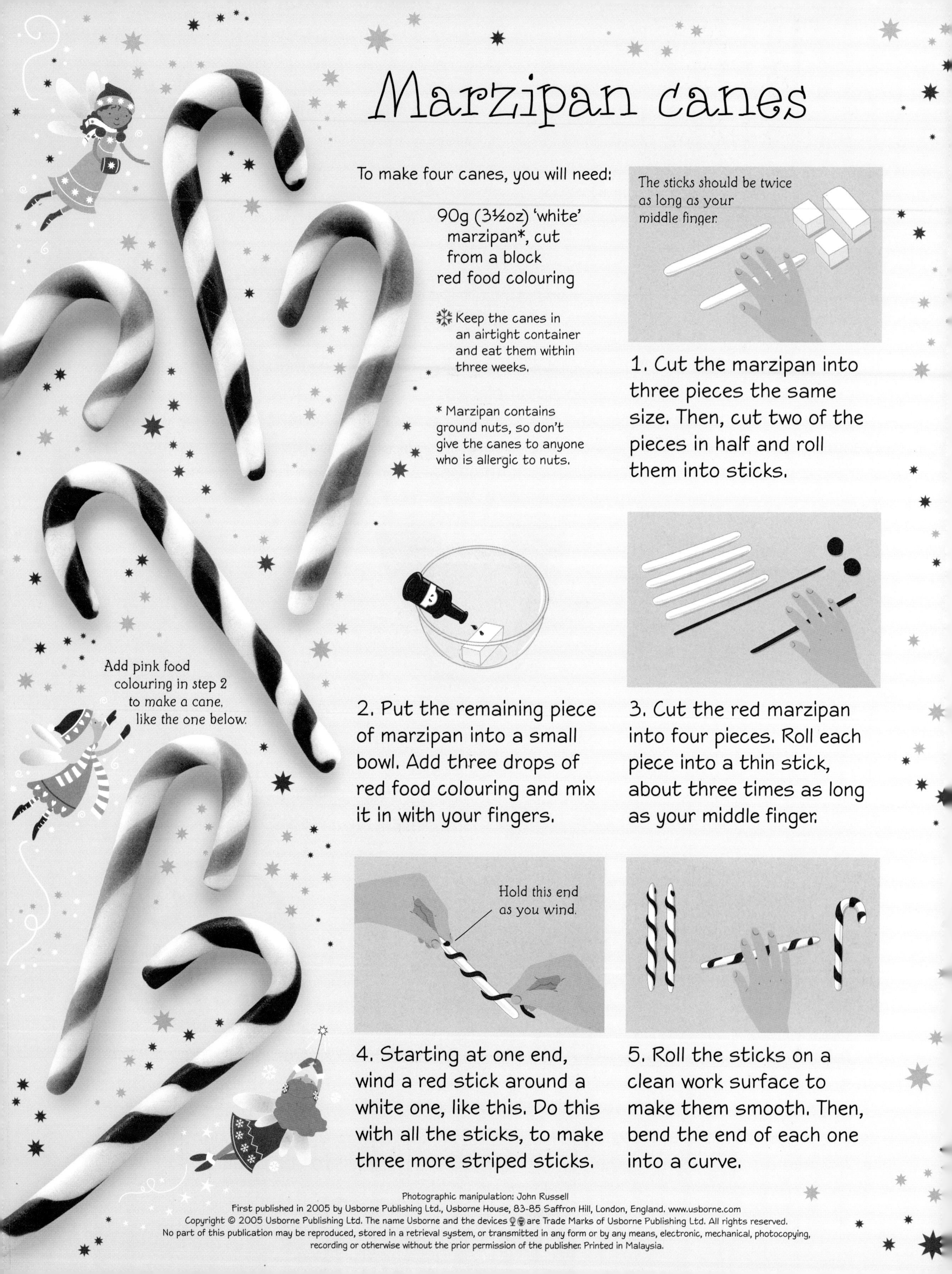

Marzipan canes

To make four canes, you will need:

90g (3½oz) 'white' marzipan*, cut from a block
red food colouring

Keep the canes in an airtight container and eat them within three weeks.

* Marzipan contains ground nuts, so don't give the canes to anyone who is allergic to nuts.

The sticks should be twice as long as your middle finger.

1. Cut the marzipan into three pieces the same size. Then, cut two of the pieces in half and roll them into sticks.

2. Put the remaining piece of marzipan into a small bowl. Add three drops of red food colouring and mix it in with your fingers.

3. Cut the red marzipan into four pieces. Roll each piece into a thin stick, about three times as long as your middle finger.

Hold this end as you wind.

4. Starting at one end, wind a red stick around a white one, like this. Do this with all the sticks, to make three more striped sticks.

5. Roll the sticks on a clean work surface to make them smooth. Then, bend the end of each one into a curve.

Add pink food colouring in step 2 to make a cane, like the one below.

Photographic manipulation: John Russell
First published in 2005 by Usborne Publishing Ltd., Usborne House, 83-85 Saffron Hill, London, England. www.usborne.com